CH00829646

SUC
SECRETS
WHICH
YOU"LL
NEVER
KNOW

MOHAMMED ARSHAD
OMER KHAN

Made with ♥ on the Notion Press Platform
www.notionpress.com

SUCCESS SECRETS WHICH YOU''LL NEVER KNOW

Success itself is meant to be a secret..

The more the failures the higher the levels of success

Contents

ONE

INTRODUCTION

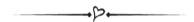

I've created this super amazing success guide after years of pain and learning. In this amazing all inclusive brief ebook, I will reveal to you simple steps to be joyful, successful & healthy. Success isn't just about being rich, there are richer things than just being rich. There are more precious things than a luxury car, a mansion & money. There are things that you may have but the rich don't.

I believe you can be cured of cancer and you can overcome financial loss, depression & failed relationships. You can be successful, healthy and happy again.

The No.1 reason that people suffer from failure and diseases is because of UNHEALTHY LIFESTYLE & EVIL SOCIETY.

No.2 Reason that people suffer from diseases and failure is because they aren't eating HEALTHY. YOU CAN FIGHT ANY DISEASE JUST BY CHANGING TO A HEALTHY DIET & HEALTHY LIFESTYLE.

LET ME TELL YOU AN UNTOLD SECRET :

DO YOU KNOW THAT COWS DON'T GET INFECTED WITH HIV AIDS. DO YOU KNOW THAT RAW ORGANIC COW MILK HAS A GREAT POWER TO CURE ALL

DISEASES. A COW THAT EATS FROM ALL GREEN VEGETATION HAS THE BEST MILK. NATURAL RAW COW MILK & NATURAL RAW HONEY HAS A GREAT POWER TO CURE. BUT THAT'S IF YOU AVOID POISONOUS FOODS THAT I'VE MENTIONED IN THIS E-BOOK FURTHER. SOMETIMES WHEN YOU ARE ILL YOU MAY HAVE TO STOP ALL HIGH SUGAR FOODS, BECAUSE HIGH SUGARY FOODS WILL FEED THE BACTERIA AND VIRUSES. BUT IF YOU FEEL TOO WEAK, EAT FRUITS IN MODERATE QUANTITIES OR DRINK NATURAL FRUIT JUICE. YOU MAY ALSO MAKE DELICIOUS VEGETABLE SOUPS. AND DRINK RAW ORGANIC COW MILK MORE.

You can find more about this in the websites below :
https://www.statnews.com/2017/07/20/cows-vaccines-hiv-immune
https://time.com/4865239/how-cows-are-helping-fight-against-hiv/

DISCLAIMER :

1- MAKE SURE TO GET MILK FROM A HEALTHY COW

2- IF YOU HAVE A SERIOUS CONDITION, DO CONSULT A PROFESSIONAL DOCTOR AND A NUTRITIONIST OR A DIETITIAN

3- TAKE MEDICATION AS PRESCRIBED BY THE DOCTOR AND ALSO CHANGE YOUR DIET AS PER THE NUTRITIONIST'S ADVICE.

NO MEDICINE WILL BENEFIT YOU WITHOUT CHANGING YOUR DIET, SO DON'T EXPECT TO GET CURED FROM MILK OR HONEY IF YOU DON'T STOP TAKING THINGS THAT ARE HARMING YOU

TWO

RELATIONSHIP BETWEEN HEALTHY FOOD & SUCCESS ?

Healthy food is very important for your success. Just imagine you are the richest guy on earth but you have a deadly disease and nobody wants to come near you. You are sick and nobody likes you. Wouldn't you want to buy health with all the money you have ? Certainly you would. So if you are healthy that means you are really really rich. Remember the biggest wealth you have is time & health.

Eating Healthy doesn't mean that you have to eat fruits and veggies all the time. You can have a burger, you can have a pizza too, you can enjoy your delicious foods But you have to change a few of your ingredients.

E.g. If you love bread, then go for a whole wheat bread. If you can make a whole wheat bread at home then that's the Best Way to go.

E.g.2 If you love milk, then consume Raw organic milk in moderate quantities, don't buy that crappy pasteurized UHT treated MILK. Go to your local farmer, tell him to milk the cow and just drink it. The more you heat milk, the more it loses it's natural properties.

ALL FOOD IN IT'S NATURAL FORM IS HEALTHY ,

Eating is not the problem, but eating PROCESSED FOODS is. So make sure your food is organic and raw.

Eating Fried Foods isn't harmful BUT the quality of OIL in it. If you are eating "REFINED OIL" then, do some research on it, you will abandon it right away.

Remember all types of Processed & Refined Foods act like slow poison. People will tell you it differs from person to person and all the crappy Philosophy, they"ll realize it when they are moving into the early 40's.

So all these refined processed foods are harmful for all ages, don't think it's just you who needs to eat healthy food. But your family needs too. If you are a meat lover then go for barbeque or grilled. Because this is very delicious and healthy.Eat as you like, just replace processed foods with organic, natural and raw food types.

DISCLAIMER

If you have a serious condition you must first consult a doctor and a nutritionist first.

If you have any disease or any medical condition or any disorder, you must consult a doctor first.

Join Our Free Telegram Group to connect with the author : https://t.me/scbguide

THREE

VISIT A PROFESSIONAL NUTRITIONIST

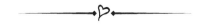

Most people visit a doctor when they're sick and then take some medications and then forget everything.Remember what you EAT is What YOU'LL BECOME. So after 40 years you don't want yourself or your children to face diabetes, hypertension, thyroid problem etc....

So visit a nutritionist, make sure to visit an experienced Nutritionist, Don't just depend on one nutritionist, take advice from two to three. Some of them may be outdated with their knowledge.

Brown rice is an unprocessed form of rice. And white rice is a heavily processed food. So the latter is very harmful. Likewise whole wheat brown flour is healthy and refined wheat flour is harmful.Even people with lactose intolerance can DRINK MILK. They can't drink processed milk. But raw milk in moderate quantities is fine.

Processed foods are very harmful , stop them or replace them with healthy alternatives. You can ask your nutritionist about healthy alternatives. I have made this ebook brief. Because time is the most important thing we have. Also make sure to look for a nutritionist that recommends Healthy organic food. If your nutritionist says to consume low fat milk, then you should know that low fat milk is a heavily processed food. It's a completely unnatural form of milk. Remember this principle : THE MORE PROCESSED THE FOOD IS THE MORE HARMFUL IT IS. So you may even advise your nutritionist, or consult other nutritionists who are more aware of processed foods

FOOD ALLERGIES :

Many people suffer from food allergies, they don't know which food is causing them allergic reactions. There are many symptoms of food allergies, just search in google to know more about food allergies. Ask your dietician too.

The Greatest DOCTOR is THE NUTRITIONIST, in another way your best doctor is your DIET, you can survive the worst of diseases if you are eating the right diet. So make sure to find a local nutritionist or a dietician and get a diet plan for a long term. Eat a wholewheat burger, meat fried in unrefined natural oil. Drink raw unprocessed milk. Replace white sugar with honey or brown sugar or jaggery. Learn how to make sweets with honey.

DISCLAIMER

If you have a serious condition you must first consult a doctor.

If you have any disease or any medical condition or any disorder, you must consult a doctor first.

FOUR

WALK FOR AN HOUR DAILY OR LEARN A SPORT, HORSE RIDING, ARROW SHOOTING, SWIMMING

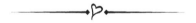

Walk Daily, Walk for an hour daily, if you can't walk for an hour, walk for half an hour. But the most effective way to keep your weight in control is to walk daily for an hour , a brisk walking style. This is the easiest exercise, don't go for extreme hardcore gym and heavy exercise except if you're interested , be moderate in everything. Don't become an extreme gym maniac, don't do steroids.

Remember the harder you are going to be on yourself, the weaker your resolve and the sooner you are going to quit. So go for easy simple exercise, don't overdo it, so you want to continue doing it for years to come. In addition, walking helps you to think more clearly, walking in peaceful places makes you calm and relaxed. You get many productive ideas when you are walking.

Get involved in good sports like horse riding, swimming, arrow shooting, so you are busy and don't have time for crappy friends.These are grand sports, KINGS DO THIS.

Don't waste your time on PC games etc...AVOID ALL VIOLENT SPORTS like BOXING, WRESTLING, these evil sports harm more than benefit. You don't want to lose your eyeball or get a twisted nose. BOXING is such a harmful sport, you'll find many boxers suffering from mental, cognition problems, brain damage etc...you can search about boxers' health problems on google or youtube. Some great boxers also end up being handicapped AND PARALYZED.

FIVE

AVOID EVIL FRIENDS, EVIL SOCIETIES (Most Important Step to a Healthy Successful Life)

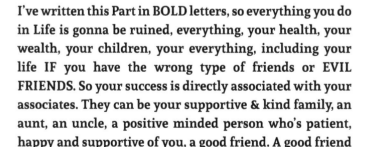

I've written this Part in BOLD letters, so everything you do in Life is gonna be ruined, everything, your health, your wealth, your children, your everything, including your life IF you have the wrong type of friends or EVIL FRIENDS. So your success is directly associated with your associates. They can be your supportive & kind family, an aunt, an uncle, a positive minded person who's patient, happy and supportive of you, a good friend. A good friend is the key to success and a bad friend is the pitfall of failure.

So the people around you, your immediate family, relatives, neighbors, all of them have a role in your development. If you are successful then remember there was a parent always behind you, there may have been an aunt, don't forget your siblings, your wife. Success only happens in a team. So make a good team.

No one in the world can claim he is a self-made man. No one. It takes years to make a man. Remember you could barely walk, talk, you were nothing. Your parents did everything for you until you were able to be successful. Your teachers, your relatives, your friends, the positive mindset of special people who were close to you all this has a great role.

Even if you practice your diet, you exercise daily, you have a good life and a good wife. But if you don't avoid those regular smokers, wine drinkers, evil negative people. They will be grinning at you, busy to destroy your morale.

Sometimes your biggest enemy is your own family. If you don't feel comfortable in your home, if you become angry all the time because of of your dad, mom or some close relative. Avoid them, go find work and live somewhere else.

You will become LIKE YOUR FRIEND. Or ATLEAST YOU"LL BE IDENTIFIED BY YOUR COMPANIONSHIP. So if you are sitting with thieves, people are gonna suspect you naturally. If you are sitting with those smokers, you are inhaling really toxic gas which pukes from their evil mouths.

Find Healthy Societies, healthy places, safe places, healthy sound minded people. Positive people. SO CHOOSE THE RIGHT FRIENDS. IN FACT THIS IS THE

FIRST STEP TO A SUCCESSFUL HEALTHY LIFE.

You may have heard of depressed people dying in accidents, committing suicide, drug abuse, greed, all this comes from evil people. Sometimes you find your own family pressuring you to earn more and more, and then you end up taking loans, losing money in useless fluctuating stock markets, gambling, just to make your dad or your girlfriend happy. Don't live with these people. I don't tell you to boycott your family or abandon them, I just say to stay away from them , live and stay in some other apartment, But you can visit them and help them, if you feel comfortable and safe. What I'm trying to say is TAKE CARE OF YOURSELF FIRST, if you are able to do that then think about others.

Angry people will make you angry, happy people will make you happy, you will become like those who you spend time with. So carefully choose with who you spend time with. The more you spend time with a person the more you are gonna be associated with him. Turns out he's a fraudster or a gangster, alcohol abuse, or behavioral problems, you are gonna get that into you because you are spending time with him.

So choose your friends and who you spend time with carefully. Because you don't want to be pursued by the police or lawyers, investigating you about your friends. This is REAL.

So if you want to live a happy free life, then avoid criminal minded people, stay away from them. In fact, this is the biggest disease. Evil society. So now you know and understand how important this affects your life.

SIX
CHECK YOUR POSTURE

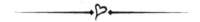

How you sleep, how you stand, how you walk , how you sit , all this is very important, if you don't have the right posture, for a couple of years nothing is gonna happen but once you are into your 30's or 40's , you'll find increasing back pain, neck pain etc....You may find out your twisted spine in your XRAY. SO maintain correct postures. Natural Postures.

IF you are sleeping on SOFT MATTRESS, then abandon it now. Sleep down on a good nice carpet on your floor. Mattresses sink in with weight, so even though you feel comfortable, after a couple of years you may start experiencing back pains. Modern Lifestyle has many comforts with secret side effects too.

Many people are suffering from back pain, neck pain, other body pains, they go to doctors, chiropractors, they get treated and then they may still experience these problems. So solving the root problem is very important. Our bodies need to rest on ground. You may buy a good floor mat. Try to sleep on it, get into a habit. The more natural lifestyle you will live the more you are going to become healthier.

SEVEN

HOME REMEDIES & ALTERNATIVE TREATMENTS

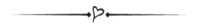

If you are not seriously ill, then the first thing to do is to try home remedies, alternative treatments. There are many health practitioners out there like cupping therapy, chiropractors, leech therapy, and many alternative treatments. Try UNANI medicine which is ancient herb medicine in India, you may try AYURVEDIC Medicine.

However if you are seriously ill, then YOU MUST CONSULT A PROFESSIONAL EXPERIENCED DOCTOR FIRST.

So generally, always consider alternative treatments. Sometimes doctors don't have solutions. Alternative treatment does....

NOW HERE I WANT TO SHARE SOME POWERFUL FOODS which you must consume daily :

1- RAW ORGANIC HONEY

2- RAW ORGANIC MILK (A COMPLETE FOOD)

3- YOGURT

4- NATURAL UNREFINED SALT

5- DATES (ENERGY FRUIT)

6- FIGS (Best Multivitamin Fruit)

7- GINGER (The Powerful Root which is found in every kitchen)

8- NATURAL SPRING WATER OR WELL WATER PURIFIED WITHOUT CHEMICALS (In India we get candle filters, we use it to filter water) USING EXTREME TECHNOLOGY TO FILTER is gonna filter out much needed MINERALS TOO.

Nobody tells you about this in this much detail BUT now you have found my guide. So make sure that the WATER you are drinking is NATURAL, SAFE, PURIFIED WITH HEALTHY PROCESSES. This may require you a little bit more research as I don't know healthy water sources in your region. It is your duty to find healthy water and give healthy water to your family.

EIGHT

AIR & LIGHT VENTILATION IN YOUR HOME, SAFE ENVIRONMENT

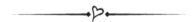

Remember the place where you live is your home. So the environment around you, the space around you, the air, light, water, people, sounds, animals. All this matters a lot. Make sure your home is sufficiently ventilated. There should be air ducts which allow fresh air and light to come in.

Avoid dark colored walls. Avoid areas where there's an air of violence, fear. Leave and abandon those wicked places. Make sure your home is in a safe place. There must be peace of mind. If you feel threatened or unsafe, contact the local authorities or police. But more importantly leave evil places, because if you live in an evil neighborhood, even the police can't do anything. Imagine how many complaints you are going to make ? Even the police are gonna be tired of you. And criminals commit crime before the police comes. Remember the police act only after the loss or crime has happened. So after that once you lose something or someone, you can't bring them back ever. So that is why leave evil neighborhoods, and move to safer, healthier neighborhoods. The world is a big place, big cities, big towns and villages. Take your first step, move to better places.

NINE
THE SUGAR CONSPIRACY

Last of all I would end here Now and I would like you to carefully read this EYE OPENING article ,

"In 1972, a British scientist sounded the alarm that sugar – and not fat – was the greatest danger to our health. But his findings were ridiculed and his reputation ruined. How did the world's top nutrition scientists get it so wrong for so long?

by Ian Leslie

Robert Lustig is a paediatric endocrinologist at the University of California who specialises in the treatment of childhood obesity. A 90-minute talk he gave in 2009, titled Sugar: The Bitter Truth, has now been viewed more than six million times on YouTube. In it, Lustig argues forcefully that fructose, a form of sugar ubiquitous in modern diets, is a "poison" culpable for America's obesity epidemic.

A year or so before the video was posted, Lustig gave a similar talk to a conference of biochemists in Adelaide, Australia. Afterwards, a scientist in the audience approached him. Surely, the man said, you've read Yudkin.

Lustig shook his head. John Yudkin, said the scientist, was a British professor of nutrition who had sounded the alarm on sugar back in 1972, in a book called Pure, White, and Deadly.

"If only a small fraction of what we know about the effects of sugar were to be revealed in relation to any other material used as a food additive," wrote Yudkin, "that material would promptly be banned." The book did well, but Yudkin paid a high price for it. Prominent nutritionists combined with the food industry to destroy his reputation, and his career never recovered. He died, in 1995, a disappointed, largely forgotten man."

Source : https://www.theguardian.com/society/2016/apr/07/the-sugar-conspiracy-robert-lustig-john-yudkin#img-4

TEN

CONCLUSION

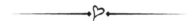

In the end, I'd like to conclude that real richness is the richness of the soul. The peace in your heart makes you rich, no matter what you earn. Maybe you earn very little, but that doesn't mean you are poor. Everyone earns according to his capability. So if you earn more then help the others, don't make fun of them because you could be in their position too.

A wise man once said "The whole earth is a bed for me, the rivers are a source of drink for me and the whole sky is a canopy for me"

Once a poor man complained about his poverty, so a wise man said to him " I want to buy one of your eyes for a million dinar", but the poor man refused to sell his eye. So the wise man said you are the richest man on earth. You have two precious eyes.

So the moral of the story is you don't have to be rich to be successful but you must learn to be content, you must live with people who are not greedy. Remember you have more precious things than just money. Your mom, your dad, your family, your eyes, so you are rich. Live your life easily. Don't be stressed. Relax. Work with positive people.

Remember your LIFE IS PRECIOUS, SO LIVE IT HAPPILY !

Lightning Source UK Ltd.
Milton Keynes UK
UKHW011329080223
416610UK00017B/2314